Joined in Love

This book of prayers has been written for couples to pray throughout their years of marriage. There are in it, however, many prayers that are living and vital for those who are not married.

The authors thank those who have contributed to special prayers with their expertise or from their experience. Her co-authors thank Alice White who also drew the inspired illustrations.

There are many other prayers that might have been included in this volume; some of these can be found in our earlier book *Linked In Prayer*, published by Collins 1987.

Reading from far left clockwise: Audrey England, Dorothy Brooker, Rosemary Atkins, Alice White, Philippa Chambers, Rosalind Buddo.

Joined in Love

Everyday Prayers for Married People

Rosemary Atkins
Dorothy Brooker
Rosalind Buddo
Philippa Chambers
Audrey England
Alice White

COLLINS

Collins Liturgical Publications
8 Grafton Street, London W1X 3LA

Available in New Zealand from
Collins Publishers, PO Box 1, Auckland

Distributed in Ireland by
Educational Company of Ireland
21 Talbot Street, Dublin 1

Collins Liturgical Australia
PO Box 316, Blackburn, Victoria 3130

Collins San Francisco
Icehouse One – 401
151 Union Street, San Francisco, CA 94111-1299

Collins Liturgical in Canada
Novalis, Box 9700, Terminal,
375 Rideau St, Ottawa, Ontario K1G 4B4

ISBN 0 00 599136 6

Copyright © text and illustrations 1987, Rosemary Atkins

First published 1988

Library of Congress Cataloging in Publication Data

Joined in love.

    1. Married people—Prayer-books and devotions—English.
I. Atkins, Rosemary.
BV4596.M3J62   1988   242′.84   87–38198
ISBN 0-00-599136-6

Cover design and typographical design by Malcolm Harvey Young.

Typeset by Burgess & Son (Abingdon) Ltd, Abingdon, Oxfordshire.

Printed in Great Britain by William Collins Sons and Company Ltd,
Glasgow

Contents

First years

Now we are more

And more growing up

Stresses and strains

Thanksgiving

Getting married, not so young

A few grey hairs

Some years on

Preface

I am very pleased to commend this collection of prayers for married couples.

When, on their wedding day, a couple takes vows of faithfulness and love 'in the presence of God and in the face of this congregation', they are buoyed up by the hopes and prayers of their families and friends. Such support is the most valuable wedding present they can receive.

Within the Christian fellowship we depend more than we can ever know on our prayer for one another, and on the way we direct our personal and private thoughts to God. Praying profoundly affects our attitudes and relationships, especially among those closest to us in our family; it gives protection against the pressures of anxiety and allows our lives to be hallowed and directed aright.

This book of prayers leads a couple through every aspect of married life: from the marriage proposal, through the birth of children, to the death of a marriage partner. It is the simple prayer which carries the greatest depth of feeling, and the simplicity and directness of the prayers in *Joined in Love* will benefit any couple who share them, and will help that couple to come to a deeper understanding of themselves, their relationship and their God.

Robert Cantuar
Archbishop of Canterbury

Will you marry me?

God of our love

Elizabeth and I love each other
    and rejoice that soon we shall marry.
We ask you
    to bless us
        in these days of happiness and smiles,
    to be near us with your guidance
        in all our planning for the future.
May our plans be realistic and considerate
    of others too,
may our hopes fulfil your will for us both,
may our dreams include your presence with us
    today and always.

Alleluia.

Learning to trust each other

Dear God,
    I've been building a shell to live inside.

        Without it

    I'm vulnerable to rejection and pain.

    Stay with me
        as I learn to open up
        without embarrassment or fear.

    Teach me to nurture our mutual trust
        by listening with care.

    With you as our friend
        we can risk ourselves with each other
        enabling our love to deepen and grow.

15

Where will we get married?

My parents expect us to marry in church.
I ask the question - why?

We haven't made this decision yet.

God is part of all the world:
      why not in a garden or even the Registry Office?

It's our marriage.

Yet Lord,
      we want to start our married life
          from the best possible place.
      We want you to be part of it.

God, you are creator of the world and everything in it;
      be in our decision making.
      As we ask for your blessing
          may we choose the place that best reflects your
          presence for us.
      Help us not to allow tempers to flare.
      May our wedding day be a day
          of joy and fellowship,
          of love and unity.

Getting to know each other

It's exciting getting to know each other better
      all the time, Lord.

I really thought I knew .... so well
      and then the other day I discovered
      he can be a real softie
          in a way I never thought *he* could.

He even remembers the same *children's stories*
      that I remember.

Thank you for that day we spent laughing together
    over small things like that;
        it was one of the best days of my life.

I know it won't be all like this, God;
        there'll be things about *him* that will irritate me
                and things about me that will irritate *him*,
    but I pray that as we get to know each other
            we will,
                with your help,
                be always tolerant and loving.

Should I have a white wedding?

God, you know I am not a virgin,
    but I want a new beginning.

    Do I get married in white?

    Should I?

    I don't know.

    I am proud to be marrying ....
        who loves me
        and respects me for who I am.

Lord God, I am to be his bride
    and I want to look radiant for him.
    Whatever I choose
        we will stand quietly before you
        and make our promises
        with sincerity and with joy.

The wedding is getting near

God, the wedding is getting closer,
    my dress doesn't look as though
        it will ever be ready.

I'm beginning to wish we'd gone
    to some far away place
        to get married
            and told everyone later.

No, I don't really-
    but all the fuss is making us jumpy.

Mum's so worried about the wedding list
    and who'll be offended if they're not asked.
I'm sorry about the argument we had over that.
Please help us to see each other's point of view.

Dad's pretty quiet, it's not quite his scene;
    he's worried about the cost;
    he didn't appreciate my suggestion
    to leave out his business and club friends.

I love my home and family
    and right now,
    please help us all
    to see the important things that need organising
    so that we can enjoy the preparations
    and have

        a truly wonderful wedding day.

Contraceptives

Creator God,
      Thank you for making us co-creators with you.

Now we come to ask you to be with us as we decide
      whether or not to use contraceptives.

There are so many things to consider Lord,
      life's pressures, finances, the size of our family.

We know so little and the options are many,
      I.U.Ds, the Pill, vasectomy and there are others.
Only you know what they might do to our bodies.

Help us to ask for advice where things are not clear.

May our decisions be for the very best motives
      and not just selfishness or the easy way out.

You ask us to play a part with you
      in making your world
            a place of people living in harmony and love.

Guide us and be with us as we decide
      how to be part of your creativity.

Who makes the decisions?

God, you made us in your likeness
      you created us male and female
      you willed that we should be together.

Fill us with your guidance,
         with your spirit of truth and understanding
            as we work through
            questions of decision-making.

Teach us to share our concerns sensitively
         with each other,
      always to speak the truth with love.

May we each honestly comprehend and accept
    the changing roles of men and women
    and their new education for living.

With your wisdom and help
    may we learn to recognise each other's expertise
    regarding decisions which we must make.

May we know
    that if we ask
    your Spirit will give us always
    a right judgement and a wise decision.

Her parents and mine

All these years
    we've been their children
    loved and protected.

Now they're uncertain
    about our future.

        Loving God
            please give them
            confidence
                in our decision.

As our lives grow together
    we want to show your
    love
        like ripples
            expanding
                in a pool
                    to encircle
                        our separate
                        families.
                Then we will all
                    be enriched.

Have I made the right decision?

Next week I'm going to marry ....

I do love *him*
> but I'm beginning to panic.
>> Will I be trapped in a situation
>> from which there is no escape?
>> Do I want to spend the rest
>> of my life with ....
>> How much give and how much take?

Calm me Lord
> so that I can be rational.

God, I do love *him*
> and we've decided to marry.
> I pray that we will accept our
>> separate and joint responsibilities
>> within our marriage.
> Help us to see our wedding
>> as a new beginning in our relationship.
> Help us to know
>> that we must continually work at it.

Our priorities will change.

It won't always be easy.

Give us the vision to recognise
> that what is worth having
>> is worth working for.

Thank you for this time of quiet
> to get everything back into focus.

I panicked.

> You have given me peace.

Second marriage

In the stillness of this moment

I hold my breath

and marvel at the wonder

of this second chance in marriage.

God, thank you for this second time of marriage.
We each accept all that has gone before.
We pledge ourselves to this new love.
May our experiences and differences
take on a positive value,
that through them we may enrich our lives
as we learn from one another.

Thank you for our past,
for the pains and
for the joys.

Thank you for your blessing on us now.
May we continue to know this blessing
and may it always be part
of our lives together.

Mixed marriages

Lord Jesus, I've read in the Bible
that in you there are no differences
in class, race or colour.

So .... and I come to ask you
to bless our marriage.
We come from our different ....
(race, religion, denomination, culture)
and we've come feeling hurt
from the rejection of others.

But we've come with our eyes wide open
    knowing it will not always be easy
    and that people will watch and wonder.

May we never take each other for granted.
May we continue to learn
    from each other's tradition
    and may our different backgrounds
    bring new flavour and new richness
        into our home.

You are a God who is beyond limitations.
You are love and your love is without prejudice.
May our marriage reflect
    your love and
    your acceptance of us.

We now want this union to be for ever

We have made the decision.

We want this union to be forever and
    we want it to be witnessed and blessed
    by our families and friends.

We are in a sense already married
    but now we realise what was missing
    to make it really whole.

Lord God, be with us as we prepare for our wedding.
    Forgive our impatience and
        our thoughts only for ourselves.
    May we grow from the mistakes we have made
        and bring to our wedding day
        a complete commitment to each other.
    May our love for each other be blessed by you
        so that from our shaky start
        a strong and lasting relationship will grow.

We ask this through Jesus Christ our Lord.

I'm pregnant and we're getting married

.... and I have decided to marry.

I'm pregnant, but our decision is for the right reason –
we love each other.

Creator God,
we thank you for the wonder of creation.
You give us free will and yet
you also give us guidelines to live by.
You are a God who understands our frailties.

Forgive us now.

We are excited as we think of this new child
which is ours
growing inside me.

May we give to our child
a home of love and security.

Our decision to marry
has come sooner than we planned.

Be with us in our preparation.

Be with us in the months ahead.

Children – How many?

Jesus you were part of an earthly home
and knew the joy of a family.

We come to you now and ask for your guidance
as we decide whether to have children
and how many.
We are made in your image and children
are part of your gift to us.

Part of having children
is to accept responsibility for another person.

And yet Lord,
sometimes what we decide doesn't happen.
Please help us then not to be jealous of others.
May we keep things in perspective
and be open to new directions.

May what we decide always reflect
your love,
your care,
your plan for us.

May our home be a haven
where children and adults alike
may find peace and serenity.

He's not my child

Creator God,
thank you for the love .... and I share
and for the excitement of a new future together.

.... already has a child
whom I love very much;
he's not my child
but I pray *he* may accept
and love me
as a true and trusted friend.

There may be moments
when this situation
creates its own special problems,
so I pray for all the wisdom,
love and
tolerance
necessary to
overcome them.

Wedding nerves

We are quite overwhelmed
    with all the flowers
        good wishes
        gifts
        and everyone being so kind.

It seems so strange
    to be the centre of all this attention.

We want a lovely wedding
    but it seems to involve so much.

Tensions are mounting
    and it's hard not to become confused and upset.

O God,
        let us take a pause,

        to be still,

        to feel you here with us.

Take away all these wedding nerves.

Fill us with confidence and assurance;
    confidence to make our vows and the
    assurance of each other's love.

We pray that all who join
    in the celebration of our wedding
    will receive your blessings of love and joy.

Our wedding day
and our honeymoon

Thank you for this day

Loving God,
    our friends have shared our love today
      celebrating our wedding,
      blessing us with their joy.
        Thank you for their love.

    So many people have shown they care,
      they've worked so quietly on our behalf
      to give us this memory.
        Thank you for their support.

    Their thoughtful presents will help us
      build our home together,
      a tangible record of this day
      and of the special love
      with which we are surrounded.
        Thank you for this day.

I'm glad we said 'no'

I'm glad we waited
    until our wedding day
    with all the joy of anticipation,
      the wonder,
      the freedom.

Thank you God for the strength
    to do what we knew was best
    which makes us free
      to enjoy this moment
      of commitment and love.

Tonight our bodies share in love

Creator God,
Creator of our lives,
Creator of our love;
  Today our words gave witness to the world
      of the love of our hearts and minds.
  Tonight our bodies give witness to each other
      of the passion and longing of that love.

  May we be
      sensitive to the needs of each other,
      learning how to delight and to caress.

  May we be
      strong in gentleness,
      tender in newness,
      patient in uncertainty,
      growing in understanding,
      caring always for our bodies
          for they are the temples of your Spirit.

We have time together - at last

Jesus, in your earthly life
    you knew the necessity
        of times of quietness,
        of times of being away from the crowds.

  In recent weeks,
      we have found great joys and some
          frustrations
      in all the busyness and planning,
      in all the comings and goings
          that filled the days before our wedding.

  Now we have time together - at last,
      time to share our love
          in the total giving
              of our bodies to each other;

time to relax and to caress,
    to talk and to be silent;
time to unwind from all the pressures,
time to rejoice in the love you have given us.

May we use this time well,
    so that when our honeymoon is ended
we may be refreshed and renewed,
happy to take up our tasks in the world,
strong in the unity
of the love and the friendship
    which binds us together.

It's reality now

Dear Jesus,
I feel in some ways we've been organised into this,
not quite strong enough to go against the current
and quite enjoying all the fuss.

But it's reality now and there's no turning back.

This *man* I've married is like a stranger.
I have no passion,
    only fear on our wedding night.

    It's alright Lord, we'll make it work.
We know your love for us both.
Without expectations we may be more fortunate
    than others with a romantic vision.
Show me how to love *him* truly,
    not to be afraid of rebuffs and cold shoulders;
    I know they come from
        his own sense of inadequacy.
    If I respond in kind we reinforce our difficulties.

Stay with us Lord in our need.

Honeymoon blues

Help me Lord!

Why isn't it working?

Suddenly we seem like strangers.

I suppose we've never been alone so long together.

We've run out of things to say.

When it all went wrong in bed last night
    he wouldn't talk about it.

O Lord, please help us,
    this is the start of our marriage
    and we do want it to work.
    Help me to talk to *him*
        and may *he* know the need I feel
        to have *him* talk things through.

He's an owl and I'm a lark

Help us Lord Jesus to compromise,
    for *he's* an owl and I'm a lark.

His sense of humour often hurts
    yet I know *he's* only teasing,
    taking the mickey out of me.

Teach us tolerance
    for traits different from those we're used to.
Help us to build strength of character
    blending these differences into a lasting bond.

Love is bigger than these petty things.
Love never fails.
Thank you for our love for you and for each other.

God bless her

I had no idea,
    she squeezes the toothpaste in the middle
    and leaves her shoes everywhere.

But she tidies the newspaper
    when I've messed it about.
    She puts flowers on the table
    and she sings in the shower.

God bless her.

I don't like
    some of *her* friends

We are man and wife.

In your presence Lord
    and by your minister
    we were married.
We promised
    to support each other,
    to care for each other,
    to love each other.
Our friends rejoiced with us
    and will include us in their social activities.

Some of *her* friends I'm not keen on.
Some of my friends *she* does not like.
We don't always enjoy each other's interests.
We have to learn to give and take.

Loving God,
    help us to respect each other's likes and dislikes;
    give us the grace to be patient,
                    tolerant,
                    understanding,
    that we may each be our own person
    and yet
    one.

He's been married before

O Lord,
   thank you for the happiness
      we share today on our wedding.
   May the joy and love we now know
      grow through the years and see us through
      difficult and good times together.
   John has been married before
      and I know there was hurt
      in that part of *his* life.
   Thank you for the opportunity our marriage brings
      to overcome the past and build a happy future.

God be in our home

Jesus of Nazareth,
      born into an earthly home,
   come in the power of your Spirit
   and be always with us in our home.

   When we work -
      give us your strength for our tasks;

   When we relax -
      give us your peace for our renewal;

   When we argue -
      give us your self-control for our help;

   When we celebrate -
      give us your joy for our rejoicing;

   When we are weary or concerned -
      give us your love and your wisdom
      to uphold us.

The contrast is so great

It's all so different now!

After all the weeks and months
of preparations and excitement
now it's just .... and me.

We love each other dearly
but now our horizons seem bounded
by our daily living, our jobs, our home-making.

The contrast is so great!

Loving Jesus,
angels and kings heralded your birth
but then, in the security of your family
and your everyday living
you prepared to be the Saviour of all people.

Teach us to treasure these days
for they will bring us fullness of life together.
May we learn to make them special
with a bunch of flowers
or a meal lovingly prepared.
Equip us in these quiet days
for our journey in love together,
that we may be confidently ready
for all that the future holds.

Each marriage is unique

O Lord,
John comes from a home
where his father is 'man of the house'
and makes all the important decisions.
My background is different
and I believe in having an equal say
in the decision making.

Thank you for *John's* easy going nature
and for the love we share
which makes it easier to discuss these things.

You created men and women
to be partners.
Lord, help us to find a true partnership.

Sometimes together, then apart

We both love tennis
to watch and to play.
But what of rugby,   office,
choir,   sewing,   painting,
music,   fishing.

We need to find a middle stream
so we can sail quite free
along some hidden waterways,
then merge together, bubbling, strong,
with all we've gathered on our way.

Lord Jesus,
help us as we go
to build our lives
unselfishly,
sometimes together,
then apart,

but blending all
in a splendid whole.

Fitting all our lives together

Lord Jesus,
>   it's hard to put our jigsaw together,
>   I feel my part isn't fully represented.

>   Is it because my work is unpaid?
>   As he is the breadwinner has he higher status?
>   Are my friends and my work less important?

>   Help us to be more careful
>   with each other's personhood.
>   We each need the other's respect
>   to build our roles at home
>   and in the wider world outside.

>   Please help us to grow as individuals
>   affirming our uniqueness.
>   Teach us to look after each other's friends
>   and to make friendships with those
>   who value us both.

>   The special gifts that you have given us
>   will fill our jigsaw with colour and life,
>   interlocking our lives with bonds of love.

To work or not to work?

I want to understand my role more clearly.
I'm feeling suffocated by my confinement to the house
>   and yearn for a place in the world.

I don't want my vision narrowed down.
I don't want to be grumpy about things
>   that aren't important.

What should I do?
Can I manage a dual role?
Is it right to ask for help to share the home load?
Will it put my marriage at risk?

Lord Jesus, you gave women stature and confidence,
    I trust you now to help me choose.

I'm earning more than *Andrew*

I'm used to being able
    to buy the things I want,
    to go out to restaurants,
    to plan holidays and outings;
    but it hasn't been like that for *Andrew*.

Now we must plan and save
    for our future,
    for our home,
    for our family.

'Money talk' can so often cause great hurts.

May we acknowledge that as the talents and skills
    that we possess, are gifts from you,
    so the money we earn is also your gift to us.

God, our creator,
    help us to be sensitive and honest,
        and to understand each other
        when we talk of our money
        and how best to use it.
    Together may we learn to use our money
            wisely and well,
            honestly and generously,
        offering always our thanks
        for your goodness to us.

Our decision is not to have children

Why do I feel
    as though I have to explain myself?

It's a decision that .... and I have made.

O Lord,
    our decision not to have children
        has been made for the best of reasons.
    As husband and wife together
        we know that we can make a home
            that is both loving and welcoming.
    May we share our talents
        and bring them as gifts to our marriage.
    In developing our individual interests
        may we enhance our relationship
            and learn to give and take.

Your money and mine

Lord God,
    guide us as we plan our finances.
    We have each controlled our own incomes
        and now we must share,
        and it won't always be easy.

Grant us the honesty to accept
    both our individual and our shared priorities.
In all our decision-making
    we want to put you first.
In all our living,
    may our money be a blessing,
    not a burden.

Making a will

We've been told we ought to make a will.

We hadn't thought of that.

Lord God, we are young
    and dying isn't something we've thought about;
    yet it's thinking of all aspects of our life together
    that's part of sharing love.
    Thank you for the reminder by *Robin*
        to look at this important task.

    May we remember that in the years ahead
        we need to stop,
        revalue
        and bring things up to date.
        Then burdens will be eased
        and tasks made lighter
            if one of us should die.

    Bless our lives together
        and bless those who remind us
        of important jobs for living.

How shall our *house* become a home?

Lord, how shall we furnish our *house?*
    It isn't very big.
    It isn't very beautiful.
    But how shall we make it a home?

We have some lovely gifts,
    the practical ones are already in good use.
But there are so many spaces
    and so many possessions that we'd love to own,
    things that our families and friends
    almost seem to take for granted.

But how shall our *house* become a home?

It isn't very big,
>   but love takes no space.
It isn't very beautiful,
>   but joy can transform everything.
The lovely gifts add beauty
>   and your presence Lord gives us peace.

Those family ties

There are times Lord
>   when I need *his* help,
>   when I want *his* company,
>   when I plan an outing for two;
>   and then *he* says *he* must
>>   write to
>>   or be with
>>   or do something for *his* family.

God, you gave us to each other,
>   you bless our marriage with love.
>   May .... and I be secure enough
>>   to understand
>>   and to share between us *his* responsibilities
>>   and the demands that are made of *him*.
>   May we also learn that sometimes we must say 'no'.

My new in-laws

Thank you God for my in-laws.

I feel so much part of their family,
>   the welcome they have given me,
>   the times and happiness we've already shared.

May our love and friendship continue to grow.

In-law troubles

Are there any couples who don't have in-law troubles?

Lord,
> I've reached the point where I've got to make a stand.

> *Terry's* mother wants to be part of our lives.

> Well yes, I know she is part of our lives,
>> but she wants more than I can give
>> and I find myself boiling over with irritation
>>> which I can't manage to express.

> Please help me to deal with this pent up anger.

> I've let it all pour out to *Terry*
>> and I know I've hurt him.
> I've said stupid and vindictive things
>> which haven't helped at all;
>> they've just made him rush to protect her,
>>> in the same way that I do
>>>> if he criticises my family.

> Please help me to stand off
>> and see things in perspective.

> Give me courage to say what I believe,
>> wisdom to say only what is necessary,
>> love to say it kindly,
>> real forgiveness to try again.

Where will we be for Christmas?

A celebration needs people
> and Christmas is a family celebration.
Each Christmas is different
> but the message is the same.

Help us, Jesus,
    not to turn your witness of peace and joy
    into a time of strife and sadness
        as we plan our preparations
        and wonder where we will be.
    Both our families have expectations of us
        but we need to be free to choose,
        and free to give.

Bless us all this Christmas.

My mother always did the dishes

My mother always did the dishes,
    she always made our beds,
    she always cleaned our shoes,
    she always cooked the meals.

Why can't *Mary* do those things?

Why won't *Mary* do those things?

Why should I help?

Why should I bother?

Hey!   No!

But she's working too, in her job,
               in our home,
    with our children,
    with their friends,
  and I love her,
    I love her very much.

Lord, help me not to be selfish,
        not to make comparisons,
    but to happily share the tasks with *Mary*
  knowing that as I care for her
    she is also caring for me.

I'm fed up

I'm in a rut!
  we don't do anything anymore.

Our whole life revolves around this house -
  painting, paper-hanging .... Yuk!

Lord help me to get things back into perspective.
  Help me to find the excitement and the thrill again
    of creating something which is ours.
  Give us the occasional nudge
    so we will stop and take time out together,
    so our marriage will always contain
    the flavour and newness of life.

First row

Words   words   words
  battle on like a storm raging,
  each gust attempting to outdo the last
  until, exhausted and spent,
  only destruction is left.

Words, wisely spoken,
  coming from a loving heart
  with clarity of thought,
  these are the words that achieve the heart's desire.

O God our Creator,
　　we've decided that stormy words
　　are not for us again.
　　They did no good and hurt us both.

　　We forgive each other,
　　　　please forgive us too.

We ask you to help us as we try
　　to think more clearly,
　　to speak honestly with each other,
　　to state our needs and desires
　　　　with clarity and gentleness,
　　　　　　for Jesus' sake.

I hear them say ...

'She's not pregnant yet' I hear them say.

'When are you two going to start a family?'

'How soon can we expect to hear the patter of tiny feet?'

'*Mary's* expecting her first soon!'
　　　　　　And so it goes on.

That's our business Lord;
ours and yours.

Forgive me when I get angry
　　but these remarks make me furious.

We do want a family.
We look forward to having all the fun,
　　frustrations and fulfilment
　　we know that children can bring.

Whatever our family will be
　　it will be blessed by you.

It's not easy to work together

It's not easy to work with ....,
    she's a slow thinker whilst I'm quick.
I'm fired up in the morning
    whilst *she's* groping out of sleep;
    and I need to sleep when *she's* awake.
Working and living together
    it's often easy to be irritated.

We've shared our lives in every other way.

Lord help us to work this out.

We're privileged to have this time together
    but we need to plan time apart too.

Let us see, with your eyes, each other's value.

Where do I go to find someone to talk to?

When I say my marriage is just wonderful,
    I know I lie.

It's the expected response, but it's hollow.
I've read the books
        but they don't really answer my questions
        and *John* finds it embarrassing.

Where do I go to find someone to talk to?

Please Jesus help us,
    teach us to see your gift of sex as one
        among all your wonderful gifts.
    Let us be honest and
        let love be in our talking
        as we share our needs compassionately
            with each other.

    Give us the courage to seek
        the counsel and guidance we so desperately need.

I'm not giving her the pleasure she hopes for

We've been married a while now
    and I don't think I'm getting it right.
I'm not giving her the pleasure she hopes for.
She says it's O.K. but I know she's disappointed.
I'm feeling inadequate Lord.

Why?
Why is it like this?
Why is the total unity not there?
    We are trying so hard
        but it is not there.

Maybe we're trying too hard,
        hoping too much,
        feeling too tense.

Wait!   Stop!

Do I need to take time?
  - time to admire her dress,
  - time to share a meal,
  - time to tell her I care,
  - time to listen and to hear,
  - time to relax and to caress,
  - time to dream our dreams,
    time to trust,
  - time to delight,
  - time to love
    in our fullness.

I am *Mary Jones*

We've been making some mistakes
        in our relationship Lord.
I've been thinking of *John* as *my husband*
        and I've had unreal expectations
            of what this should mean.
I've really resented *his* expectations of me as *his wife*
        and the role I'm meant to fill.

I am *Mary Jones*.

I'm good at my job
        and I have many interests;
            some I share with *John* and others I don't.
I don't want to give up the things I enjoy
        and I shouldn't expect *John* to either.

Help us to recognise the wholeness of each other,
        to grow together without imposing expectations,
        to grow as individuals without being selfish.

She does not share my faith

God of Love,
    she does not share my love for you,
    she does not know
        the freedom that comes from trusting in you:
        the freedom from fear,
        the freedom to abandon all cares and anxieties
            into your hands;
    she does not know
        the peace and serenity of your presence,
        the assurance of your divine love;
    she tolerates my 'religious' activities.

Lord, whether or not *she* accepts you
    is between you and *her*.
Grant that my love for you
    will not be a threat to *her*.
Grant me the wisdom to live and love
    so that *she* will want to share
      my knowledge and faith in you.
One day, dear God,
    may we walk with you together.

We've been longing
for a baby

You know
    we've been longing for a baby.
You know our disappointment
    as the months went by.
When my body
    began to feel different
      we were afraid
        to hope too much.

Now we know for sure!

The first time I felt sick I was glad
    but I'm not so thrilled about the sickness any more.
Three months they say and it usually goes away.
Three months seems a very long time
    so I ask you Jesus to help me
      through these early days.
Please protect our unborn baby
    and help me to go about my daily life with a smile.

As I give up work to prepare for our child

Loving Creator,
    as this gift of love grows within me,
    I thank you for the privilege
        of nurturing a new creation.
    As I give up work to prepare for our child
        may I eat, rest and exercise wisely.
    Help me to be understanding of *Sam* and his feelings
        as my body and my personality change.
    Help him to be understanding of me.

Dear God, I thank you for the peace and serenity
        of your everlasting arms.

Will my baby be whole?

Dear Lord,
    I have had this nagging fear
        that our baby won't be whole.
    I know it's not rational,
        there's no reason to be anxious,
        but I'm still afraid.

I know there will be the skills and the strengths,
        the people and the courage,
    to deal with any situation
        but that doesn't seem to help.

Lord, you teach us to trust that you will be there
    with your everlasting arms to support us,
        come what may.
    Thank you for your presence with us.

I want him to be there

Two weeks to go before our baby is due
     and I do want .... to be there.

We both do.

Creator God,
     your gift of creation is so beautiful;
     thank you that we are part of it.

  May these next few days
       be days of rest and contentment
       and a time of sharing
       as we wait for this new life
       which is a part of us.

Now we are more

It isn't that bad being a Dad

Nine months is a long time waiting,
    but these moments are the hardest.
The thumping in my heart is nothing
    to the pain of childbirth -
    but it's hard enough for Dads.
If only it was all over
    and those words of reassurance heard
    'Mother and baby are fine!'
Why do we fear when God's love is near?
I know I shouldn't, but I do.

What did they teach her?
    relax, breathe deeply,
    pray with anticipation when the pain comes.

                Here comes another!

God, Creator, Sustainer, Giver of life,
    hold her!
    calm her!
    control her!
    give her confidence in your miracle of life!
    give me strength to give serenity to my dear one.

                Nearly there!

Yes Doctor, did you say it's a *boy*?

Wow!!

Thanks God!

        Thanks darling!

            It isn't that bad being a Dad!

Thank you God for the gift of our child

It's unbelievable!
    -the uncertainties have gone,
    -the fear has gone,
    -the pain has gone.

Our child is born!

Our child,   conceived in love,
                your gift to us.

Thank you God for the gift of our child.

Already we love *her* so much.

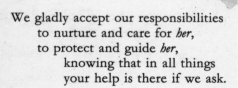

Make us good parents
        loving and wise,
        happy and just,
        joyful and strong.

We gladly accept our responsibilities
      to nurture and care for *her*,
      to protect and guide *her*,
          knowing that in all things
          your help is there if we ask.

From one father to Another

Creator God,
> as I share the joy of new creation
> > in the birth of our baby
> so I feel the weight of my responsibilities.

Lord, did you ask yourself
> 'Can I cope with it all'
> when you created the world?
> Did you wonder how you would relate to a new being
> > with a personality and will all of its own?
> Did you tremble at the thought
> > that it might threaten the relationship
> > > within the Trinity?

Lord, I tremble with fear as well as joy!

Will it be the same between my wife and me
> when she is busy with baby?

Will we have time for loving
> when we are so occupied with our new love?

Father God,
> as a father
> it has been good to share these thoughts in prayer.
> Help me to draw on your infinite love
> > to embrace my larger family
> > > with newborn love.
> Keep me steady in anxiety, steadfast in care.

If you can cope with all creation
> > then I can cope with just one newcomer
> > to bind with joy into our family circle.

So from one father to Another:

> Thanks for the opportunity!

Our adopted baby

God, source of life and love,
    we thank you for this new child,
    not born to us but given to us to love
        and to call our own.

Be with *Richard's* birth mother.
May she know peace and strength in her decision.
May she have the assurance that we will love
    and care for this baby
        so precious in your sight.

As *Richard* grows and asks questions
    may we always be honest and open.
May our home be a place of
    friendship and outreach,
    acceptance and love.

There are times when I need to say 'No'

There are times when I need to say 'No' to ....,
    when I do not want or need
        the act of physical union.

Compassionate God,
    may I show that I love *her* dearly
        and always be honest and caring;
    may I be sensitive to *her* feelings
        and never let *her* feel rejected or unwanted.
May our marriage be one where we are friends
    as well as lovers
    where we feel secure and loved.

May we recognise
    each other's need for inner privacy.

Our baby's place

God of all,
    our baby is so small and helpless
    but it could easily claim too much.

    Help us to ensure our baby doesn't take us over,
        one of us diligently caring,
        the other on the outer.
    The joys and cares are for us both to share
        and take a turn.
    Then, one of us is not worn down with care,
        while the other feels left out
        and seeks elsewhere for peace.

    Each of us is different to our baby:
        she has a special smile for each.

    God, thank you for entrusting *her* to us;
        please help us all to do our best for *her*.

We offer our child for baptism

Lord, joyfully we offer you *John* for baptism.
    May we faithfully keep the promises
        we make on *his* behalf,
        that through our living and our loving
        he will know your love
        and grow to know and love you.

A little jealous of their new half-*brother*

Lord, my children are a little jealous
    of their new half-*brother*.
    I know it's normal,
        and this sort of jealousy exists with children
            in every family;
    but stepmothers and stepfathers
        have a difficult image to overcome
        and it's not always easy to handle,
            especially now.

He's so beautiful, this baby of ours.

We are thrilled with *him*
    but help us both to be lovingly aware
    of the other children's feelings,
    so they can enjoy and love their *brother*
    in the sure knowledge
    that they too have our love and attention.

Naming our child

What name shall we give our child?

Susan Belinda or Emily Jane

      Rosalind or Philippa

            Alice or Anna.

So many alternatives.
So many meanings of names.
So many suggestions from others,
      from families,
      from friends.

There are family names
    and we are asked to continue them.
My family is forgetting that names cannot come
    from *our* side only.

We argued about names last night.

Wait!

This naming is becoming a worry not a joy.

Jesus, named by God,
    named for adoration,
        guide us as we choose the names for our child.
    You will know *her* by *her* name.
    May *her* name bring *her* joy,
          throughout *her* life.
    May *she* come to praise your name
      and show forth your life
      in *her* living of each day,
         for your name's sake.

It's tiring being a new mother

O please God hear me!

I just don't feel myself these days.

I can't manage to keep the house how I like it,
    and then I feel dreadful when someone comes.

I am boring to everyone and myself.

I am forever tired and feel I look awful.

I remember that verse in Isaiah,
    'They that wait upon the Lord
        shall renew their strength,
    they shall mount up with wings as eagles,
    they shall run and not be weary,
    they shall walk and not faint.'

I know you are with me God.

I know it is a strain on my body to be a new mother
    but it is perfectly natural.
I shall trust you and feel your strength.
I shall do what I can
    and not feel guilty about the rest.
I shall enjoy this short period in my life
    which passes all too soon,
        with your help O God,
            my Saviour and my Friend.

ISAIAH 40: 31

I wish he'd share the parent role

Dear God, I am tired!
>I love my *children*
>>but I'm tired of being the one
>>who does all the parenting.
>Why doesn't *Paul* see
>>how much the *children* need him?

>Show me how to include him
>>in the fun and the responsibility
>>without forcing the issue.

>Teach me to leave some gaps for him to fill.

>Give me wisdom and guidance
>>to bring this out in the open,
>>to talk about it
>>>without blaming and without nagging;
>>>then we can be a whole family.

Who will look after our baby while I work?

You know our situation Jesus,
>why I've chosen to return to work.

You know the needs of our *child*.

We want the best care for *her*
>but really don't know where to find it.

Should it be day-care with lots of other children
>or should we find another family
>where perhaps *she'd* get more love and personal care?

As we look at the different possibilities
>we offer our concern to you
>and trust that you will give us guidance
>to make the choice where *she* will get
>>the love and the care *she* needs.

I'm starting work again tomorrow

I'm starting work again tomorrow
after .... years.

I'm excited God, but oh so scared!

I feel I'm out of date,
but they did seem pleased to see me.

May I find fulfilment in this venturing out.

Lord God,
help me to keep a right balance
between family, home and work;
help me to keep my priorities right
so our home will continue to be
a place of love and security.

And more growing up

A bigger house?

Creator God,
> *Jane* and I need to decide
> > whether or not to buy a larger house
> > for our growing family.
> May we be practical and realistic.
> May our decision not put undue strain
> > on our family and on our finances.
> May our family and friends always find
> > love and friendship
> > and a welcome
> > > in our home.

Each child is special

Creator God,

> you made us all in your image
> and yet each of us is different
> and each has infinite value in your sight.

> May we treasure our children
> > as individuals in their own right.

> They have different skills,
> > different personalities,
> > different temperaments.

> Guide us as we nurture their skills,
> > develop their personalities,
> > understand their temperaments,
> that each may be whole,
> > able to stand on their own,
> > strong in a living faith
> > > in the God who created them.

His pudding drips down through *his* highchair

Dear Lord, I'm amazed!
    This little person, our child,
        is learning, exploring, touching,
           feeling, growing, tasting,
        and it's all happening so quickly.
    Sometimes I think we have a genius
        with an outstanding future,
        but that's my ego
        and what I really want
           is to help *him* grow in balance.

His pudding drips down through *his* highchair.
I hate the mess but look at what *he's* learning,
    as *his* fingers pudge through it
    and then rub in *his* hair.
    Keep me open to where *he* is at.

He's not coordinated yet
    and I'm scared *he* will hurt *himself.*
I would feel happier doing things for *him*
    but help me to stand back
        when *he* tries on *his* own.

Show me how far to go Lord,
    to balance exploration with possible danger,
    to let *his* curiosity lead to understanding
        while I keep *him* from harm.

Thank you for these wonderful times
    as I watch your child grow.

First day at school

Jenny started school this morning.
Our baby, a school*girl*!

It's a proud moment and a sad one.

Watch over *her*, Lord Christ,
    in the new friendships *she* makes,
    in the challenges *she* meets,
    in the new concepts *she* encounters.

Surround *her* with your love
    that *she* will grow and develop
    into the whole person you plan for *her* to be.

Be with *her* Lord,
        be with me.

I've just left *him* at school

I've just left *Matthew* at school;
    my last to leave the nest
    and I feel a little down;
    and yet Lord,
        I'm proud to see this child reach out
        and join the others.

Lord God, may I use this extra time
    not to feel I'm suddenly redundant,
    but to look for and to use
    some new gift you have given me.
    Let me spend this time positively
        for myself,
        for my marriage,
        for my children,
      that I will grow to be strong,
        independent and whole
          as you want me to be.

Jenny's late home

Jenny has not come home from school yet
      and I'm worried!

She always lets me know where *she* is.

My imagination is beginning to run riot!

Dear God,
      help me to stay calm.
      There will be a reasonable explanation.
      If I need to do something,
          help me to act wisely.
      I entrust *her* and all my family to you daily.

Lord I trust you;
      strengthen my trust.

Why do they fight all the time?

Why do they fight all the time Lord?

It spoils so much of what we do together as a family.

Teach me when to stay out of their scraps
      and when to referee.
Give me tolerance to put up with the noise
      as they sort out their differences.
I know that's the best way for them to learn
      but it's very hard to put into practice.

Lord, help the two of us
      to live out the sort of relationship
          we want for our children.

The young are full of dreams and hopes

Loving Lord,
    you have created the young
        full of dreams and hopes for the future.
    Fill us with your truth
        that together with our children
        we may know what is right
        and have the courage to act wisely.
    Let us encourage their positive feelings
        and be enthusiastic and helpful
        as they strive for their goals.
    Then with your help
        may those things hoped for
            be attained.

Learning the joy of giving

Your gifts are all around us Lord,
     gifts of love,
     gifts of possessions,
     gifts of caring, giving people
        encouraging our *daughter*.

O Lord, I pray that *she* may learn
     to give to life,
     to give without expecting back,
     to think of others and
     to give herself to others in friendship.

    Then *she* will know the joy of giving.

May they find a faith in God

Creator of all,
     we thank you for our *children*.
     May they find
        faith which gives them peace
           deep within themselves,
        faith which will make them whole people,
        faith which will lead them to strive
           for justice and fair play,
        faith which enables them to show compassion
           for those in need,
        faith which lights the way to eternity:

    in the name of him who is the light of the world,
           Jesus Christ our Lord.

Will *she* never understand my concern?

I've been concerned for hours, it seems like hours,
     hours of fear,
     hours of helplessness,
     hours with my mind racing
          through all the worst happenings
              of where *she* might be,
              of what *she* might be doing,
              of whom *she* might be with.

I've listened to all those squealing tyres -
     is that a fire engine or an ambulance?

Why is *she* so inconsiderate?

Why can't *she* understand how I feel?

I'm not happy about some of *her* friends,
     or their friends!

God of peace,
God of understanding,
     give me now your peace,
              your understanding.

     She will never understand our concern
          if we do not talk about it.

          When we talk, remind me to listen.

Why must they play it so loud?

O God, it's not easy!

Our house is small and the walls too thin.
I bite my lip every time that machine is turned on.
The music's throbbing inanities get on my nerves!

She has a right to *her* taste in music
    but I feel overwhelmed, as if I have no say.
I've thought the house 'my territory'
    and this is an imposition.

She's so prickly and I'm uptight;
    we're avoiding the issue.
May we both be understanding and compromise openly.

Help me to remember you are with us
    as we sort out a solution.

Keep me open to change and less rigid in my attitude.
Help *her* to see things from my point of view.
Above all, dear God,
    don't let us damage our relationship.

Help me to understand their friends

Dear God,
    sometimes I want to wash my hands
        of the whole lot of them!
Sometimes when their friends arrive
    I feel like a stranger in my own home.

Help me to understand them
    even with their sloppy clothes,
        their way-out hair,
        their make-up.

Help me to hear beyond the language,
                    the stereo,
                    the roar of motor bikes,
                    the revving of cars.

Help me to accept the individual.

I have seen in each of them
        compassion, concern and sensitivity
                to the needs of others.
I have known their consideration for me.

Lord, sometimes these children of yours
        reveal qualities that humble me.

                Help me to understand them.

I was angry because I love *her*

Loving God,
        even in *her* tears and frustration
        may *she* know my love,
                    my care,
                    my concern.

May I never lose my temper
        through my tiredness
        or my anxiety.

May we set bounds of behaviour
        that are realistic for us all and
        considerate of each other's needs.

Today, I was angry because I love *her*.

Take away my feelings of guilt.

Some standards change, some do not

Creator God,
    we live in a world of instant this and instant that.
    Some standards change, yet some do not.

    May I open my eyes to see where change is needed.

Help me Lord,
    to preserve those things which never change.

    Give me wisdom and love as I teach my children
        to care for others and for themselves
        as they move out and form relationships.

    May they accept responsibility for their actions.

    May what we share as a family
      be creative rather than restrictive,
             and may we always have time to listen.

Stresses and strains

Is marriage really worth it?

In the closeness and trust of our marriage
    we expose our inner selves to each other
    and we know where the other is vulnerable.

Today I feel miserable, violated.

In anger *Paul* has deliberately used this
    precious, intimate knowledge to really hurt me.

But if I'm honest I have to admit
    I've done the same to him from time to time.

It's too easy Lord to be destructive
    when we know the other's weakest points so well.

And right now I wonder is marriage really worth it?

Without that permanent bond of marriage
    perhaps we'd be more careful
        of each other's feelings?

Perhaps we wouldn't have
    the same intimate knowledge?

Perhaps we'd hide the parts of ourselves
    we didn't want exposed
    and wear masks.

Dear God, I don't really want to wear a mask.
    In my hurt,
        help me to forgive *Paul*
        and forgive me for the times I've hurt him.

I do believe in marriage and I thank you for ours.

Give *Paul* and me the ability
    to work at loving each other and
    to express our anger without being destructive.

We come from different backgrounds

We come from different backgrounds
    but we are meant for each other.

Our love is so right.

Together we feel strong and enthusiastic.
We praise God that we have found each other.

There are those in our families who feel differently
    and so do some friends and acquaintances.
They ignore us when it suits them
    and try to hurt by the things they say and do.

Lord Jesus,
    may our love for you and for each other
    be strong and bright
    that we can work through these hurts
        and be forgiving.
    We believe that love never fails
        and pray that it will bring out the best
            in each one of us.
    You offer us the whole armour of God
        which no worldly dart can penetrate.
    May we remember to use it,
        for Jesus' sake.

EPHESIANS 6

She doesn't understand me

The gap between *Sarah* and me
    has been widening for months Lord,
        maybe even for years.

She doesn't seem to realise I need encouragement too.

All her time is taken up with the children
    and with her job.
She won't come out with my friends
    and resents it when I go out without her.

Now I've met *Helen*.
    She's so different,
        so understanding and fun to be with.
I find her very attractive
    and long for the warmth she could give me.

Lord I'm very tempted.

    It would be easy.

    It would be wonderful
        and yet it would be hell.

    Give me the sense not to encourage *Helen*.
    Keep me strong.

    I really love my family.
    I mustn't hurt them.

Help me to remember everything
    that first attracted me to *Sarah*.
Perhaps we both have gone too far
    in our separate ways.
Help us to talk about it rationally,
        to compromise,
            to discover each other again.
Help me to understand her needs
    and her to understand mine,
        so we can find again the love and warmth we knew.

We didn't think the age gap would matter

We didn't think the age gap would matter Lord.

We were in love and had so much in common.

But there are times now when I find the gap
          a   y a w n i n g   chasm.

We have different views on many things
          looking from our separate generations.
Then there are the children
          and *his* expectations of them.

Lord I ask you to be in the midst
          of our family of three generations
          and help us to bridge the gaps
               with tolerance,
               with understanding,
               with love.

I've met his other woman

God, I'm in a mess,

          hurting badly,

               muddle-headed,

                    shaky.

     I don't know where he is
          or whether he'll be back.
     I want to check on his mail,
          spy on him.
     At times I really want him to go.
     We've barriers of pain between us
          that make me want to scream!

He thinks *their* love is something special.

Bring him to his senses Lord.
Open his eyes.
There's so much at stake.
Please guard our children
 and teach each one of us how to forgive.

I'm pregnant again!

I'm pregnant again!

Why didn't we take more care?

I can't possibly go through all that again!

God, forgive me.
 I know I'm only thinking of myself,
  not of this new creation –
   your gift of love
    to be enjoyed,
     cherished,
      nurtured.

Creator God,
 help me to accept this trust
  and the assurance of your presence,
         your comforting strength,
   which will see me through
     the inevitable weariness and discomfort
      of the months ahead.

I have had a miscarriage

God of love,
God of creation,
   we rejoiced when we knew the certainty
      of our child growing within me;
   we kept calm too and took great care
      in all the physical and emotional changes
         that were happening.

   Now, after such a short time
      our hopes are dashed . . . . .

      I have had a miscarriage.

God, in your mercy
   help us to bear this loss,
   heal my hurt,
   heal my body,
   strengthen our love for each other;
   sustain our confidence
      in your presence with us
         now and always.

A stillborn baby

Why Lord!

Why?

After all those months,
   after all that pain,
   why was my baby born dead?

My body and my soul feel numb
   but still I ask 'why'?

What was the point?

I remember the first time *he* moved,
   like the flutter of a butterfly,
   slowly it got stronger
      and I felt a real bonding grow between us.

I even used to talk to *him*.

   Now there's nothing.

I don't even know how to pray
   because all I want is to have my baby in my arms
      and not even you God can bring *him* back.

O Lord,
   show me how to pray.
   I need to come to terms with this loss.
   I thank you for the love of *Mark*
      and of my family and friends.
   With your love and their love
      help me to start living again.

Postnatal depression

Why isn't life wonderful?

The other mothers are enjoying their babies
   but I can't pretend any longer!

I'm exhausted and confused!

It might be alright if *John* could take over.
He thinks women understand babies,
   that it all comes naturally.

If only this baby didn't cry so much!
If only *she* would feed easily!

O God, I long to be bonded with *her*.
   Give me the courage to seek help.

Cot death

O God,
> why did it happen?

> How did it happen?

> One moment *he* was there
> > alive and beautiful,
> > and then *he* was gone....

> > > *He'd* died.

Loving God,
> help me to see there is a purpose
> > and meaning in all of this.

> I know I've done everything right
> > but please take this feeling of guilt away.

> You are a God of compassion,
> > be with *John* and me.
> Help us to gain strength and comfort
> > > from each other
> > *and from our other children.*
> Help us to remember the joy and love
> > > this baby brought
> > > > and then to leave *him* in your care.

> In Jesus' name we pray.

Infertility

I never thought about infertility.

Having children seemed so natural.

Now I know I never will.

But I want to grow a baby,
    to give birth and love,
    to spend energy as a parent,
    to have a place in the creative chain.

I've found myself in supermarkets
    watching mothers and babies.

O God, the future looks bleak —
    I feel deprived of my expected role
        a lesser being for not functioning as I could.

    I'm angry at those who abort the results of
        casual sex,
        while I in anguish long for what they value
        so lightly.

    As our friends begin their families
        we're isolated in our barren world.

    In separating himself from my grief
        Harry could be covering his own private sorrow.

Give me courage, Lord,
    to help me through my grieving,
    to accept my denied motherhood,
    to bring me to a more realistic place
        where I can explore other facets of my life,
        so I can see potential in
            my home, my husband, my life.

Heal me Lord, I pray.

In vitro fertilisation

Lord, I don't understand all the concerns
    the legal and the medical people have
        and I probably never will.

I know we want a baby
    and this is our last hope.

It's been rough making the decision.
At times our marriage almost crashed.

We have each wondered about the other's commitment
    and still don't really understand what drives us on.

At the end of this endurance test
    there's only a small chance of success.
These injections and inspections are disturbing.
But the others here are just like us
    and our shared emotions heal us all.

Whatever happens in the future.
    we want to keep in touch with others who have
        shared our difficulties.

If a baby for us is your will,
    then thank you Lord.

But, if we must,
    help us to close the door on procreation, firmly.
Then may we take up our lives,
        not trailing anger and grief,
    but welcoming the future
        in confidence and peace.

Artificial insemination by donor

We married believing we could be parents.

It's been hard to choose this way Lord.

You created us man and woman.
>   It seems a sick joke that I am male in every way
>   but I will never know a child of my own flesh.

We can see the dangers ahead.

>   Should we explain to others?
>   Would they understand?

>   What will we tell our child?

>   We don't know the father – does that sound careless?
>   We don't know his medical record –
>   is there some hidden recessive gene?

We've prayed.

We believe you're with us.
>   As the future unfolds
>   keep us mindful of your continuing care.

Anorexia

O God,
>   we come to you as a family to ask you
>   to spread your healing power over us all.

>   Help us to overcome the tensions
>   which are causing us so much suffering.

>   Fill us with love for each other
>   within your all-embracing love.

Loneliness

I've never felt this way before Lord,
    never so isolated and alone.

It's getting worse.

There are just two of us and we've got nothing to say.
Fred's got companions in his work
    but I feel so lonely.

I've tried to talk to him about it
    but he says he doesn't know what I mean.
In the evening he reads his paper, watches television,
    while I'm so tense I think I'm going mad.
I'm afraid for the future; we're like strangers.

I'm scared to speak to people, scared of shopping,
    sometimes I can't say anything,
        sometimes I can't stop.
I feel as if I'm drowning and nobody cares,

But I know you're in this with me Jesus.
    Please show me who to turn to: I've lost my way.

I wish we had a house of our own

I wish we had a house that belonged to us
    with land we could call our own.
It would give a foundation to our living
    and walls, our walls,
        to shield us when we needed it.

God our sustainer,
    give us wisdom to know that it is people who matter,
        faith on which to base our living,
        strength when we need help and
        love to share with one another.
    Make us thankful that we can be together
        in this house which we make our home.

Why should I feel guilty?

God, there are times when I feel guilty
    when *Paul* comes home from work
        weary and frustrated,
    when the children come home from school
        hungry and quarrelsome,
    and I have spent the day doing 'my thing'.

Help me to get it all into perspective.

I have no need to feel guilty.

We each do our 'own thing'
    and together we share
        the frustrations,
        the successes,
        the joys.

Thank you God, in Jesus' name,
    thank you for straightening me out.

Sometimes their thoughtlessness riles me

I do love my family God,
    but sometimes their thoughtlessness riles me!

They expect to find cakes in the tins,
    meals on the table at times to suit them,
        and sometimes I feel that all I am
            is cook and washerwoman!

Help them to understand that I don't like doing
    the things they often take for granted.

Give me the tact to suggest how they might help;
    they aren't really uncaring;
    they're just so preoccupied with their own concerns.

Sharing is much more fun.

An accident

O God help us!

Help our *daughter*,
    she's badly hurt!

Please calm the fear in our hearts as we cling
        to your promise;
   ' ... I am the Lord your God,
    who takes hold of your right hand
    and says to you "Do not fear;
    I will help you." '

We believe you love *Sally* even more than we do
    and we need that reassurance now.
We uphold *her* to you and ask you to surround *her*
    in your healing, protecting light.

Thank you Lord for your word
    that 'through our faith our children are made holy.'

Thank you for the skill of those who are caring.

Give us now we pray,
    courage to face the days ahead,
    strength to be there when we're needed,
    faith to know that whatever happens
        Sally is yours,
           held always close to you.

ISAIAH 41. 13
1 COR. 7. 14

Our *son* has a motorbike

Caring God,
 I offer you *Andrew* and *his* motorbike.

 It is *his* pride and joy.

 Nothing thrills *him* more than to ride and ride
            and ride.

 Each day I see *him* put on
  the 'whole armour of God'
  and *his* crash 'helmet of salvation'.

 Thank you that *he* comes home safely.

 Thank you for the faith you have given me
  to believe that I can confidently
  leave *him* in your care.

 Though I may worry, I will not fear.

EPHESIANS 6

Our daughter says she's pregnant

My thoughts are in a jumble!

Surely it's not true!

How could she do this to us?

After all we've taught her,
 all we've done for her!

And yet I'll be a grandparent
 and every baby should be wanted.

What's happened to the boy?
 How does he feel?

She can't be certain!

But she is certain
    and resentful,
        and bewildered,
            and unwell,
    fearful of the future,
            for her,
            for us,
            for her baby.

Lord Jesus, you accept us all,
    may we accept our daughter now.
    May she know our love for her.
    May she show us how we can help her.

Lord Jesus, hold us all in your love.

I wait for results

God of compassion,
    be near me
        as I wait for results from my tests.

    I'm finding it hard.
    My mind's racing on.

    Still me!
    Hold me.

    Whatever decisions may have to be made,
        may I know your presence and
                your love for me.

Drugs! It can't be true!

Not *Jenny*!

God, why?

Where did we go wrong?

Hold me together God!

Give us the tact and sensitivity
    to tell *her* that we know.
Let *her* see that our love for *her* hasn't changed.

Give us the courage to seek help,
                to talk to the right people.
Give *her* the will and the strength
                to kick the habit.

God, only you can transform that which is ugly
           into that which enriches and blesses.

Help us Lord.

AIDS is a problem

Dear Lord,
    I hear so much about AIDS these days.
    It confuses me and I am afraid
        for myself,
        for those I love,
        for those around me.
    It seems a darkness is pervading the whole world
      threatening all people.
    What can I do?
    Where can I go?

I turn to you my God, for you created us
　　and sent your only Son to save us all.
You give us your word to live by
　　and your Spirit to enable us to live out your purpose.
You have never abandoned us
　　even though we turn from you.

And so I bring this problem of AIDS to you
　　with all the issues entwined with it,
　　　　of homosexuality, drug addiction,
　　　　　　prostitution, promiscuity
　　　　and those infected through no action of their own;
　　issues too complex for me to try to understand.

I ask you loving Lord,
　　to bless and guide those who are trying to cope
　　　　with this problem
　　　　so they will not themselves be compromised.
　　I pray for those who continue to place themselves
　　　　at risk
　　　　by their own actions,
　　　　that you will bring them knowledge and conviction
　　　　　　there is another way,
　　　　　　there is hope.
Your hope.　　　Your way.

I ask that you would soften my heart
　　that I might look with your compassion
　　　　on those at risk.
Let me see with your eyes their own special needs
　　and grant me the courage and strength to respond
　　　　as your Son would.

Infected with AIDS

Loving God, I bring before you ....
    who is infected with the AIDS virus.
  He/she needs your help so much
    because the future seems so bleak.

Light of the World, shine on in our darkness.
  Let your loving gaze look on ....
    and cast out all fear.
  Fill his/her heart with your peace,
    a peace the world does not have to offer.
  Touch him/her with your healing hand,
    bringing a new wholeness to mind and body,
      a new freshness,
      a new dawn to life.
  If he/she must face death
    let him/her be surrounded by loving friends.

Dear Lord,
  as I commend .... to your loving care,
  I also acknowledge my own fears and concerns,
    and seek your help in my relationship with.....
  Do not let my feelings and my fears
    freeze my compassion
    or make me withdrawn in my caring love.

Let my speech,   my touch,   my face
  reflect your ongoing love for ....

Caring Creator,
  help me to trust in the love I know you have
    for him/her
    and give me the strength and courage
    to cooperate with you in the plan you have
    for us all.

For in you, dear God,
  in you alone, do we trust.

Was that ethical?

Why did I make that excuse?
Why did I tell a half-truth?
Why did I accept too much change?
Why did I mislead with false information?
Why did I deliberately make an error to confuse?

God of truth,
    I need your forgiveness,
        your help.
    Teach me to live truthfully
        in all my words and actions.
          Then I will know the freedom that truth brings
          and be true to Christ
              my way,
              my truth,
              my life.

Menopause

God, source of all understanding,
    be with me as the changes happen in my body.

Help me to remember that
it is a normal process for every woman.

Help me to come to terms with my changing moods.
Take away my feelings of guilt when my temper frays.
Make me seek medical advice if this is needed.

May this be a time of new assessment,
    a time to look at new horizons,
            at new opportunities,
    and may I never lose sight of my part
        in your creation.

Menopause - the season of change

The season of change is here for me,
　　　this frontier between growing up and growing old.

My life was a pattern.
I fitted in so well the dictates of society,
　　　of work and home and family.
Now the tapestry is done,
　　　complete, predictably correct.

So here I am,
　　　success or failure,
　　　　　I must go on,
　　　　　　　but now, alas,
　　　there seems no path.

·O God, light my way.

Reluctantly I start another tapestry.
Amazed at what I see, my fears disperse.
Unhindered now, the pattern takes a different turn,
　　　the colours rich and rare.

A surge of joyful energy takes me to heights unknown.

My spirit uninhibited, not now restrained,
　　　finds its true self, reveals its latent soul.

　　　　　Thank you God, I have found me.

Today I was made redundant

I should have known .....

               the rumours .....

    but there was always the hope it wouldn't be me.

But it is me, O God!

I feel as if the bottom of the world has opened
        and I've fallen into
           a great
               black
                    hole.

Compassionate God,
    help me to keep
    a right perspective on it all.
    Don't let me become bitter,
    don't let me lose hope
        even as I feel
            angry,
                unwanted,
                    rejected.
    May I use this time to plan
        and not feel too proud
            to accept opportunities
                when they are offered.

May my family know the support and love
    already being shown to me.

Keep us calm
    as together we plan for the weeks ahead.

His redundancy - but

I'm hurting too!

I'm feeling vulnerable!

I want to help
    but *John* wants to cope in his way.

Our God,
    give us strength as he faces his redundancy.

    Be with us both
        as we look to the future
        with all its new directions.

I am not the breadwinner

My wife is working.

I have to watch her go out to work each day
    and I stay at home.

Why did it happen to me?

Why did I have to give up work so early?

Merciful God,
    help me to overcome my prejudice,
    to accept the fact that I am not the breadwinner.
    My role has changed.

    Surround me with your presence.
    Help me to overcome my self-centredness,
        to seek out the possibilities
            you have waiting for me.

    You want only that which is for my utmost good
        and I thank you that you are
           'My refuge and my fortress,
           my God, in whom I trust.'

PSALM 91

How will we pay these bills?

These bills ....
> they keep on coming and I'm scared!

How will we pay them?

Lord Jesus, you calmed the storm,
> you gave your disciples peace.

> Calm me now.

> We are short of money
>> and for a moment I lost all sense of
>> proportion.

> Allow us time to sit and work things out.

> May we not be too proud to seek for help.

> Thank you Lord,
>> your peace surrounds me.
> Stay with us as we sort this out.

Late home again

He hasn't come home for *his* meal again tonight!
I'm ready to throw it at *him* if *he* does.

Dear God, I'm at the end of my tether!

> Help me!

> Help me to be patient,
>> to show my hurt without whining,
>> to keep my dignity.
> Help *him* to recognise me as a person
>> and to respect my needs.
> Grant that we may listen to each other,
>> to work this out,
>> and together grow in our love.

A birthday

It's great to have a day to celebrate, Lord.

Today is ....'s birthday.
   We want to make it special!

One day can merge into another so easily.
   We need special days to add some colour
      to change the pattern.

Be with us in our celebration.
Bless ....
   as we show *him* that we care.

A wedding anniversary

God of love,
   when we married ... years ago
   we looked forward with happy expectations
   to the joys of love and family life.

   There were hurts and disappointments,
      but you healed our hurts
      and blessed us in ways we hadn't expected.
   There were disillusionments and difficulties
      but you gathered us in your loving arms
      and shared our burdens.

   We thank you God,
      for you have been constantly in our midst.
      Your still small voice speaks peace and
         encouragement.
      Together we have grown
         in love, wisdom and understanding.

      In quiet faith and confidence
         we will walk on with you together.

These certain dates of special meaning

These certain dates of special meaning to us
    are ordinary days for others,
    and ordinary days for us
        can be special days for someone else.
So when we celebrate our anniversaries
    sometimes others do not know or care.
It is between us and God.

The bitter-sweet memories flood in
    and we dare to steep ourselves
        in the sacredness of the day.

O God,
    thank you for your closeness
        to us on our special day.
    Thank you that we can celebrate
        this day of remembrance and new beginnings.
    Thank you for those to whom we are linked
        by love for ever and ever.
    Thank you for your love and peace.

God's gifts at Christmas

Heavenly Father,
    thank you for your gifts to us this Christmas Day,
        your gift of light to show the way,
        your gifts of truth and peace,
        your gift of faith,
        your gift of hope,
    and most of all
        I thank you Lord for Jesus Christ,
        your gift of boundless love.

Easter

Jesus Christ,
    by your resurrection
        you gave us the gift of eternal life.

May we take hold of that life now
    and show in our daily lives
        your joy,
        your hope,
        your peace,
        your faith,
    rejoicing always
        that we are your Easter people.

We're proud of *her* achievement

We're so proud Lord, to be able to share this moment.

We want to tell everyone we meet how wonderful *she* is
    but that would be a boring boast.

As parents we've been proud of *her* achievement
    but we've made no demands;
        our children need no certificate to earn our love.

But for now, let's celebrate this special day,
        let's glow with reflected glory,
        let's give unstinted praise
            for a well-earned reward,
        let's make this time sparkle
    so our *daughter* will have this memory
    of shared fulfilment all *her* life.

Thank you for this day when our world stopped
    and we immersed ourselves in *her* achievement.

A family day

How good it is to feel the hot sand underfoot.

We breathe deeply, absorbing the balmy salt air.

We race to the sea and dive into the foaming waves.

The tide's on the turn,
    there are shellfish to dig.
    Someone's gone for a bucket.

Oh isn't it lovely today!

The children are off to the rocks
    to search the pools for strange creatures.

We, abandoning our cares,
    stroll along the water's edge,
        our senses acutely receptive,
            fascinated anew at the bounty of nature.

O God our creator,
    for this beautiful day,
    for our wonderful world,
    for our happy family,
        we thank you with all our hearts.

Thank you for this sunset

God of all the universe,
    I watched your creation
        radiate your praise tonight,
        as sky and cloud and hills
        were tinged with light
        that deepened into orange and into flame.

    Your glory was proclaimed in all the colours
        that an artist knows.

    Your wonder was shown in the myriad of stars
        that brought the night
            to give us rest and peace.

    Tonight I thank you for the glories of your sunset.

Thank you for this moment

Loving Creator,
> thank you for this moment
>> when I know your presence,
>>> feel your hand
>> guiding my actions and my planning,
>> making me ready for new opportunities
>> and new tasks.

Thank you for your presence with me.

His family - her family

There were two trees joined in an arch.
Their roots were well established,
    their branches independent of the other,
        yet entwining;
    flowers and fruits oddly dispersed,
    breathtaking in their beauty,
    richer for their dual display..

O God,
    our later marriage is like the blending
        of those trees.
    Together in your strength
        may we be a source of love and understanding,
        the common ground
        for our young and theirs in turn
            to build on as they grow and flourish.

Where are we going to live?

God, you have blessed us abundantly
    in this new marriage.

We bring to you our past
    as well as our hopes for the future.

We ask you to guide us
    as we decide where we are going to live.
We each have a home which we don't want to leave
    but either one or both of us must make a change.

We want our home to be 'our place'
    which we can share with our families and friends.
May we be sensitive to their feelings
    and may they see that we care
        not only for each other,
            but also for them.

A new pattern of life

God of grace,
     when *David* asked me to marry him
          I wanted to say 'yes',
but, established in my career,
set in a pattern of life that I enjoyed,
what was I to say?

I knew I'd lose my

       independence

but I loved him!

I'm glad I said 'yes'.

Thank you for the blessings of our marriage.
Thank you for the friendship and support,
         the understanding and acceptance,
         the freedom to be ourselves.

Thank you loving God.

What of my career now that I am to marry?

Suddenly my life is turning upside down
and I am excited and radiantly happy!
Life has a new purpose, a new direction,
as together we plan for
our future,
our home,
our hopes for the years to come.

But what of my career now that I am to marry?

Spirit of God,
guide us in our decision-making,
teach us to communicate sensitively with each other,
help us to hear and to understand.
May ours be a marriage
where each will grow
and together fulfil
our dearest dreams, our greatest hopes.

Health check

Loving God,
in the excitement and joy
of planning for our wedding,
may we pause
and remind ourselves
that we are not young any more.
May we be responsible in checking out our health
and seeing that a regular visit to the doctor
is a way of sharing a burden
and showing our love for one another.

Today we feel young again
as we plan for our wedding.

Thank you for reminding us of our responsibility
to ourselves and to each other.

I need to accept *his* first marriage

Dear God,
    when I married *Derek*
    I didn't give much thought to *his* first *wife*
    but now that I'm living in this home
        where they lived too,
    there are little reminders which make it important
    for me to acknowledge *her*
    and the life that they shared.

Lord help me not to resent that part of *his* life,
    nor try to replace or compete with *her*.
    Give me serenity in our love and companionship
        which allows me to accept
        that part of *his* life
            which *he* shared with *her*.

Thank you God for this marriage

We bring the strengths of our previous marriages
    to enrich this one.

Bless us as we continually learn
    to give and take in our new relationship.

Thank you for your presence with us
    during the difficult times,
    working out our financial arrangements,
    adjusting to each other's habits,
    relating to our families.

Loving God, we are so blessed,
        may others share our blessings.

Rediscovering each other

Our love is different now.

There was a time when I wanted *Bill*
    to prove *he* loved me in words and actions,
    an ego-centred love.

Then Lord,
    I learnt to let go of unreal expectations,
    to nail these to your cross and leave them there,
    opening myself to be changed.

Now you have given us real companionship.

We're more honest with each other and aware.
Our bond is stronger than before
    as we live each moment fully.

Thank you for the calm and peace we share.

It hasn't always been easy

Gracious God, we use this opportunity
    to look back on our lives together
    and to give you thanks for our family
        and the years we've shared.

    It hasn't always been easy;
        there were times of great tensions
            and disappointments.

    Thank you
        that we were able to use these times
            constructively,
        for the friends who helped us see them through,
        for the love and care with which our family
            have surrounded us,
        for the strength you gave to us.

    Be with us in the years we have together,
            in Jesus' name we pray.

Sharing a new interest or A chat with God

We've never had time on our hands before Lord.
You know the busy lives we've led.
Now in our small house and tiny garden
    there's not nearly as much to do.
The grandchildren don't need us as often as they did.

So we offered to help at *the drop-in centre* last week.
Was that your idea?
There wasn't a lot to do,
    sandwiches for me to spread and *Jim* drove the car
        to pick up some who can't drive anymore.
We had a lovely day!
We talked to people we knew and people we didn't.
Jim found some toys in the creche that needed mending.
    That'll keep him happy for a month!

I'm sure we're going to enjoy our weekly turn down there.
It's given us a new interest together
    and something fresh to talk about.

Thank you Lord for leading us there.

A different generation

Dear God,
it's difficult not to feel anxious.
Our children have grown up
    in a more permissive society than we knew.
They have a different attitude to sex
    and relationships.
Should we tolerate this
    or make a stand according to our views?

We want to keep communication open
      and not to be repressive,
   but their views differ
      and it's hard to know how far to compromise.

Although they've taken responsibility
   for their decisions for a long time
      they still ask for advice.
Are they really wondering if what we believe is right?

Help us to come to terms with our young people's lives,
   respecting them as individuals,
   a different generation.

In our love we leave them in your safe keeping.

Bless *John* and *Mary*
      - a parent's prayer for an engaged couple

Lord, bless *John* and *Mary*
   who have just announced their engagement.
   We have watched this relationship grow
      and we are delighted to welcome ....
      as part of our family.
At times we had some misgivings
   but they've been resolved.

Soon they will be married.

May they learn tolerance and understanding,
      patience and wisdom.
May they always be honest with each other
   and respect the other's need for space.
Above all let them retain their sense of humour!

If our advice is sought,
   may we give it with care and sensitivity.

Now, in Jesus' name we offer them to you.

Our home is now too big

Lord Jesus,
>you are a part of our family
>with infinite love for each of us.

Our home is now too big.

We ask for your guidance as we plan to change.

As we look to the years ahead
>may we choose our new house wisely.
>The size of house and garden,
>the locality and position,
>the maintenance that will be needed
>>are all important for our future.

Be with us in our moving.

Help us as we make our new house
>into our new home for the future.

What shall we take to our new home?

Loving God,
>when you created the world
>did you have a problem of choice?

Our new house is smaller.

It already delights us
>but we'll never fit everything in!

Guide us now as we choose
>which of our possessions will come with us
>>into this new chapter of life.

Fill our hearts with gratitude for all we have,
>especially
>>your overwhelming love for us both.

Money – planning ahead

Lord, the world of finance is so confusing.
    We're concerned about our home,
        about crises of illness, disability,
        and who will help when one of us dies?
    Will we have enough money?

We've had so much advice,
        some wrong advice;
    it's very hard to know which course to take.

Figures are thrown at us too fast to take in
    and it's confusing.

But most of all Lord,
there's never enough time to understand it properly
and people don't realise we're slower now.

Please help us not to be anxious about the future,
    or too proud to ask for help.

May we live each day sure of your presence with us.

Our grandchild

Thank you God for this beautiful child,
    for *his* mother and father too.

The new parents relax now, their victory gained,
    ecstatic but humble in knowing that
        the tiny unspoiled child
        is theirs to nuture, to care for and love.

Out of their joy they are giving us joy
    and your world is continuing on.

Immortal God, ever creating fresh new life,
    as we delight in our grandchild,
    help us to show *him* true love and security,
        that *he* may see you in our lives, and follow.

They chase till they drop

They like to play computer games,
    create things with transformers,
    but
    just like their parents and us before them
    they still love to plant garden patches
    with radishes, cornflowers and marigolds.

They chase till they drop,
    puffing, laughing.

Their warm hands, vibrating and eager, seek ours.

O God,
    may we show our grandchildren
    that our strength and joy comes from loving you
    and may they learn to know you and trust you
                            for ever.

Let's travel

A trip to the other side of the world!

Why not?

Is it too much of an undertaking at our age Lord?

We're both fit and love to travel.

Our family here are a little concerned
    but our family there are very keen for us to come.

We're not so young it's true,
    perhaps there is some risk attached,
    but that's all part of living isn't it?
We'll plan it carefully and get the best advice we can.

Guide us Lord, we pray,
    and be with us wherever we go.

Tolerance

God of wisdom,
    you understand me so well.
    You are patient with me
        despite my pernickety ways.

Grant me the grace
    to show that patience to others,
    to listen with tolerance,
    to curb my tongue,
    to be prepared to admit I'm wrong;
        then the harmony of our life together
        will continue to mature in your love.

Extra time

What extra time?

Loving and generous God,
    you have opened so many doors to me,
        my days are full.

Thank you for all my new interests,
    for the old and new friends who enjoy them with me.

Thank you for my contemporaries who share my memories,
    for the young who accept me and make me young.

I marvel at the bounty of your gifts.

I revel in the beauty of your creation;
        the parks,
        the gardens,
        the countryside,
        the sight and sound of children at play,
        and music.

Thank you for the tears and the laughter.

Life is so full of joy, dear God,
    that my heart sings in praise to your glory.

May *she* know our presence now

Loving God,
    be near us with your strength and your peace
    as we wait and watch with *Mother*
        as *she* journeys from us to *her* eternity.

May *she* know our presence and our love
    until *she* comes into the radiancy
        of your presence
    and knows the certainty of your love for *her*.

Into your everlasting arms
    we commend our dear one.

Retirement

One door is closing,
    another doorway beckons.

Dear God,
    soon there will no longer be
        that daily rush to work;
    soon we will be able to plan our time freely.

Gracious and loving God,
    with your Spirit to guide us,
    we can plan for a future that will enable us
        to live our retirement in contentment
        and in the constant awareness
            of your presence.

I do miss my job

Lord, I do miss my job.

    Give me a new purpose in life.
    Help me to see that I have a part to play
        and have not become worthless.

    Allow me to open new doors,
        to keep my eyes wide open for new opportunities.

    May these retirement days be for *Mary* and me
        a time of rediscovery,
            of new ventures,
            of new friendships.
    May we not allow creaking bones and greying hair
    to cloud the purpose of living in these later years.

    Be with us both.

He's under my feet

He's left his papers all about the house,
  taken the milk bottles away in the car,
  forgotten to bring in the firewood as he promised.

It's driving me crazy having him here all day!

My life was so efficient Lord,
  orderly and running smoothly;
    now I can't find things
    and everything's in a mess.

This house of ours has always been 'my territory'
  but I need to accommodate his style
    and I'm having trouble.

I wonder how he feels?

Please help us get this in perspective.

Show us how to plan with honesty,
  to enjoy the freedom
    from the confines of our working days.

Remind us how fortunate we are
  to have this time together.

Spending wisely

O God, we praise you for supplying our need.

  Help us to spend our money wisely
    budgeting for real needs week by week,
      for nourishing food to savour and enjoy,
      for things providing extra warmth
        and safety,
      for the occasional taxi ride, hair do,
        pedicure or gift.

Thank you God,
    that with care
    we can afford these things
        and enjoy the pleasures that they bring.

We have time to enjoy each other

Loving Creator,
    it seems as though you've given us a second chance.

    After all these years
        of busyness, of deadlines,
        of demands, of other's concerns,
    now, in our retirement,
        at last we have time with each other.
    We can enjoy the privilege of planning each day
                        - guide us as we plan.
    We can relax and take outings together
                        - restore us in these times.
    We can take up new hobbies and new interests
                        - be near us as we choose.
    May our retirement be a time of re-creation
        and in all we do may we know
            your presence with us,
            your love surrounding us to eternity.

Time together

Thank you God for time to be together,
    to do some things we've always wanted to.

Our garden is now a stunning picture,
    our work and care producing plenty
        for others and ourselves to share.

There is always something new
    for us to study and explore,
        somewhere where we can sow some seeds of joy,
        someone with whom we can share your love.

Thank you God
    for the eternal rebirth in your creation,
        so that when we work together with nature
            we can look forward to the harvest.

Creaky bones

Almighty God,
    we are getting old and sometimes I'm afraid.
How are we going to cope?
With our creaky bones
    even little jobs like changing light bulbs
        are dangerous for us now.
If either of us has a fall or becomes ill
    what will we do?
        Who will look after us?

You are our strength in times of need O Lord.
Help us to accept change if change is the answer,
        assistance when we need it,
    and to live each day to the full
        caring for each other.
Thank you for the comfort you give
    when we bring our cares to you.

I sit and drift at peace among my memories

What a panorama opens up before me!

Dear God,
      how wonderful it has all been,
            the families,
            the friends,
            the places,
            the experiences.
     There were some unhappy times,
         but your constant love bound us together
             healing us,
             comforting us,
             giving us courage to go on.

Gracious and loving God,
     thank you for the memories,
              for the serenity your peace brings.
     Thank you for whatever is to come.
               I am at peace in your love.

He can't do all that *he* could

Loving God,
     it grieves and worries me to watch ....
     He can't do all that *he* used to.
     He won't accept the limitations of age
        but *his* legs fail *him*, *he* forgets things,
       he tires easily and *he's* fretting.

Grant me the patience not to snap and argue,
         the wisdom to be encouraging,
         the strength to be supportive.

Grant us both
     the peace that passes all understanding,
     the peace that is serenity, O God.

I feel hesitant to leave *her* alone

Photographs in frames,
    informal pictures of places,
        celebrations, people smiling,
            capture precious moments of the past.
Thank you God for those great times now gone.

Thank you too for present days together;
    we have your love and comfort with us still
        and feel quite satisfied.
We save the seed of zinnias for the spring
    and marvel at the cheek of sparrows pecking crumbs.

But *she* cannot go out
    and I feel hesitant to go out on my own.
I know I should be mixing more.
I could perhaps *play bowls* or *learn to sketch*
    and bring some fun and freshness home with me.

O God our sustainer,
    help me as I seek
    to find an interest that will benefit us both,
                    for Jesus' sake.

He's so muddled

Loving God,
    I ask you to still the panic in my heart
        as I stand by and watch helplessly
        while *Les* becomes more remote
          and more muddled.
I'm so afraid of losing *him*.
Has *he* gone on an inward journey?
That's how it seems Lord
    and I don't know how to cope.
We've always been close and shared so much
    but *he's* not the same person any more.

Give *him* peace of mind,
    he sometimes struggles so.
Help me always to remember the good times
    and the *Les* I used to know.

Dear God, I ask for peace,
    your peace to overcome my fears.
Thank you for my faith.
    Give me courage
        to accept what comes.

Afraid of death

God of hope,
    there are moments when the fear of death
        sweeps over me like a wave.
I'm afraid of life without *Joan* should *she* die first,
    and I'm afraid of facing my own death.

You are the God of love,
    help me to let go all the fears, resentments
        and hurts I cling to.
Help me to trust in you
        and put my life and *Joan's* in your hands,
        in the knowledge that Jesus will be there
                on the other side
        waiting for each of us
            with outstretched arms;
                    in his name I pray.

I cannot manage *him* any more

God, source of all help and guidance,
    be with me in my decision.
John has become a burden
       and I cannot manage any more.

I can't cope!

Take away my feelings of guilt.
Take away my feelings of anger.
      These people will take care of *John*
         better than I can.

I know my feelings are irrational,
    I'm told it's part of a grief process.

Be with me.

May I remember *John* as *he* really is,
    funloving, witty and so proud of *his* family.
May I always see under this crippling disability
    the *husband* I love.

Be with *him* and with me
      as we reach out our hands to those who offer
        loving help and compassion.
Let us see in them your Son
    as he comes to be with us in our need.

I need their help

Lord Jesus,
    before you died you gave your mother Mary
      into the care of the beloved disciple.

Did you know that Mary would need
    the support of a younger person?

Did you know that John would need
and find fulfilment
in giving her his strength?

I need help now,
help with the daily chores,
help with the decision-making,
help with financial matters.
May my family and friends have the love
and understanding
to help me without making me feel helpless,
to guide me without making me feel stupid,
to support me without making me feel unable.

Thank you for your love and understanding of me,
always.

Help me to be grateful for their care

Compassionate God,
it's hard to see younger family and friends
doing all the tasks for me
that I was happy and proud to do for myself.

Help me to be grateful for their care and
to thank them;
may I not make unnecessary demands for time
or attention.

May I always welcome their embrace with a smile
rather than begin our meeting
with a list of tasks to be done.

May I remember too their other commitments
with families and friends.

Thank you for my family
and for your presence with me
in the times I am alone.

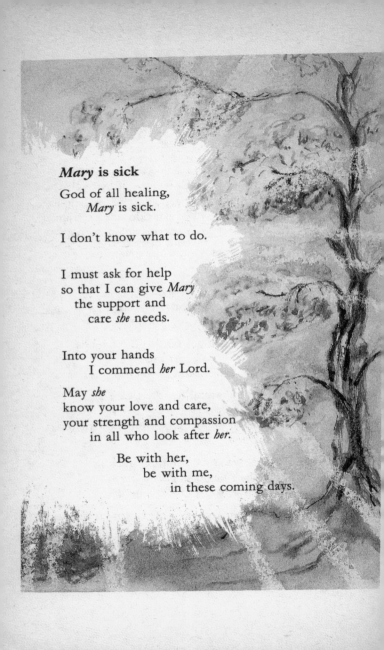

Mary is sick

God of all healing,
  Mary is sick.

I don't know what to do.

I must ask for help
so that I can give *Mary*
  the support and
    care *she* needs.

Into your hands
  I commend *her* Lord.

May *she*
know your love and care,
your strength and compassion
  in all who look after *her*.

      Be with her,
        be with me,
          in these coming days.

Joined in love

My God,
    my *husband* has died.

I'm now alone
    and I want to thank you
        for those wonderful years.

It wasn't always easy
    but in your strength we saw it through.

I know your power and your guiding hand
    as I journey on.

I am continually assured that *Peter* and I are
    joined in love,
        your love, which lasts for eternity.

Each new day I praise you,
    confident that in your care

        I am not alone.

LINKED IN PRAYER

Everyday prayers for everyday people

Rosemary Atkins and others

Fresh and spontaneous prayers, arising from the joys, sorrows and tragedies of family living – prayers that link us with God and with each other.

Prayers written by a number of women and young people in New Zealand, that reach out to men, women and young people in every part of the world

• About the life and growth of the family: the birth of a new child

• For all sorts of people in all sorts of situations: a single parent, a moment of panic

• Personal prayers: help in redundancy, for facing family violence

• For times of need: making a decision, facing up to breast cancer

• For celebration and thanksgiving: preparing for marriage

• Prayers by young people for young people: for exams today, loneliness

'...covers so many facets of family life and...has been produced with great imagination and love ...will fulfil a great personal need in the prayer life of many families.'
President, Mothers' Union

COLLINS

ISBN 0 00 599996 0